My Sister,
My Friend

Having a sister
   like you . . .

      is like having
      a friend and a
      smile and a
      rainbow
      all rolled into one.

               — Laine Parsons

My Sister,
My Friend

A collection of poems
Edited by Susan Polis Schutz

Library of Congress Number: 82-70270
ISBN: 0-88396-172-5

Manufactured in the United States of America
First Printing: March, 1982.
Second Printing: April, 1982.

The following have previously appeared in Blue Mountain Arts publications:

"The love of a family," by Susan Polis Schutz. Copyright © Stephen Schutz and Susan Polis Schutz, 1980. "My sister means so much to me," "Our Family" and "There are so many things," by Andrew Tawney; "You mean so much to me," by Jamie Delere; "A sister like you . . ." and "Sometimes I get lonely," by Laine Parsons. Copyright © Blue Mountain Arts, Inc., 1981. "Having a sister like you . . ." and "You're someone that I think about," by Laine Parsons; and "Sometimes I think," by amanda pierce. Copyright © Blue Mountain Arts, Inc., 1982. "Thinking of home," by Louise Bradford Lowell. Copyright © Continental Publications, 1978. "Thanks for listening," by Miles M. Hutchinson. Copyright © Continental Publications, 1979. All rights reserved.

Thanks to the Blue Mountain Arts creative staff.

ACKNOWLEDGMENTS appear on page 62.

Blue Mountain Press INC.

P.O. Box 4549, Boulder, Colorado 80306

CONTENTS

My Sister, My Forever Friend

You have always been
        my true friend.
The fact is not
that I will always
have you near me,
but that you will always
        be near me . . .
in my heart.
Forever
is a binding word,
but I do care for you
        in that way.
Above all else in life,
I find for myself
what's most true
        through knowing you.

So no matter
what time brings,
always know that I love you.
I'm so glad
you're my sister . . .
I'm so thankful
        you're my friend.

— Janice Lamb

To be blessed with
  a wonderful sister

I ask myself
why I have been
  blessed with someone
  so understanding
  and so caring . . .

Perhaps it's because
I can truly appreciate you
or maybe it's because
  God knew
  I needed you
  so much.

— Jean Therese

For my sister

As we grow older
I learn to appreciate you
        more and more.
When we were just children,
we had our disagreements,
      which was only natural,
but even then I knew
that you were a very special friend.

Throughout the years
you have shown me affection
and have always been there
when I needed someone.

Together we have shared
      secrets, laughter
and the joys of growing up.
And in that time
I hope that I have returned to you
some of the love
you have unselfishly given to me.
I am forever grateful
to have a sister like you.

— E. Lori Milton

My sister means so much to me
and though I hardly ever let her know,
I think of her most every day
and feel her glowing love

My sister means so much to me
for I cherish the life we have lived
We have come to know
the true meaning of sharing
and have come to grow
in the light and warmth
of the family bond

My sister means so much to me
when I think of the sweet days gone by
when I think of the good times
we've yet to unravel
in moments beyond today
in places along the way . . .

My sister means so much to me
   when I need my dearest friend
   I know whom to turn to
   I know whom to trust
   I know who will hold me
     with her gentle, loving touch

My sister means so much to me
   I want her so to know
   I'd like to give her
     the best of everything
  for she gives
    so much
      to me

— Andrew Tawney

I am thankful for the opportunity
    to have grown up with a sister like you.
It helps me to remember that
the close, loving relationship
    that we now share
was forged from childhood
and through growing together.
In maturity I have come to realize
how special a sister can be.
For there is no one else who knows you
    better
for what you once were, and what you
    still hope to be.

— Marilyn Wallace Luff

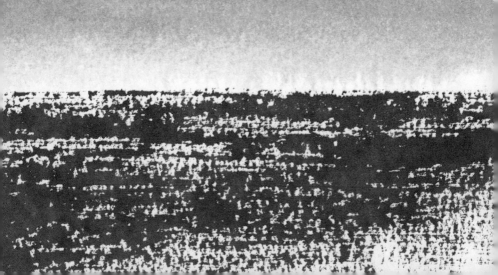

I wanted you to know today
that you are especially on my mind
and in my prayers.
You are such a beautiful, loving person.
You give so much of yourself to others.
I pray that God's many blessings
will be yours — today and every day.
You are a blessing to so many, and
I love you very much.

— Jan Kirkley Boyd

Sometimes the pressures of life,
    the worries and frustrations
build walls between us.
You see things your way
    and I see things my way . . .
and for a short time
we forget what we really mean
        to each other.

Through patience and understanding
    the harmony is restored,
and we can share life's beauty
        together again.

— Susan Staszewski

Having a sister as a special friend

It is comforting
to know that we are friends;
that we can share our thoughts
        with each other in confidence,
that we can listen and care
        for each other with love
                and concern . . .
It makes my heart glad
        to know that we are friends.
And I want to tell you
        how much I care and
        how often I am thinking of you.
Have a wonderful day,
                friend.

— Doris Amundson Arnold

You mean so much to me —
  and I just wanted
  you to know
  how very much I care . . .

You mean so much to me —
  you've helped me to find
  a special outlook on life
  that was hiding
  deep inside of me,
  waiting just for someone like you
  to open the door
  and set it free

You mean so much to me —
  for you've been there,
  through the good times and the bad,
  drying the tears and
  holding back the loneliness —
  giving me a friendly shoulder
  to lean on
  and enough smiles to last a lifetime . . .

You mean so much to me —
    and I can't help but feel
    as though I owe you so much more
    than I can ever repay
    But if there's a way —
    any way
    to hold and to help,
    to provide and to encourage,
    to give even a part of what
    you have blessed me with,
    I will be there for you

And wherever time will take us . . .
    wherever we may be,
    I always want you
        to remember
    how much
    you mean to me.

                              — Jamie Delere

Remember, sister . . .

If ever you need to talk,
    to share a laugh,
    a dream, a smile;
to be comforted
or reassured,
to be understood . . .

Remember,
my shoulder is there
    for your head,
your secrets are safe
and my door
is always open.

— Ronda Scott

If I could, sis . . .

I'd like to capture a rainbow
and stick it in a big box
so that,
anytime you wanted to,
you could reach in and pull out
a piece of sunshine.

I'd like to build you a mountain
that you could call your very own
a place to find serenity
in those times when you
feel the need to be
closer to yourself . . .

I'd like to be the one
who's there with you when you're
lonely or troubled
or you just need
someone
to hold on to.
I'd like to do all this and more
to make your life happy.

But, sometimes,
it isn't easy to do
the things I would like to do
or give the things I would
like to give.

So . . . until I learn how to
catch rainbows and build mountains,
let me do for you that which I know best . . .

. . . Let me simply
be your friend.

— Jacqueline J. Hancock

When the world closes in
and lies so heavily upon you . . .
remember that I care.
When the ones with whom you
share your life seem strangers . . .
remember that I care.
When love seems to only bring
you pain . . .
remember that I care.

What cannot be, cannot be.
But always remember, I care.
Never be afraid to come to me,
if you have need of the simplest thing.
No matter what it is . . .
                    I care.

                        — Kathy Boss

We may take
different steps
on different paths,
we may get caught up
in different aspects of life,
we may not be able
to touch and to share . . .
but our love
  will always
    be there.

— Sheryll Anne Sneade

Sometimes I think you're about
the best friend
        a person could ever have
Other times, I know
you're much more than a friend
You are an important part of my life
that I carry with me
        wherever I go, and
whether you are near or far,
        we are always together.

                                    — amanda pierce

When I'm away from you

You're someone that I think about
so much —
wondering how you are,
and hoping that you're happy.
I just wanted
to remind you
(in case you've forgotten!)
how much you're appreciated
and how very much
you're missed.

— Laine Parsons

Wherever people go,
whatever they may invent,
they will never discover
   anything better
than a family.

— Paul Gauguin

My Family . . .

There is an
irreplaceable feeling
that I wouldn't give up for the world;
a sense of belonging,
of being able to turn
to the outstretched hands
        of those I love . . . at any time;
to know they'll understand me,
        and comfort me
        when things go wrong,
or laugh with me
        when things make me happy.
Caring and sharing
        life's ups and downs,
and mostly
        loving . . .
as I so dearly love them.

— Debbie Avery

The time I have with you
Is very special.
To reach out to you
And know you'll be there —
That means all the world to me.
My heart is with you
   wherever you go,
My love is yours no matter what.

When you smile at me,
I know it's from your heart.
I know you'll do for me
What no one else would do.
And if I don't tell you
I love you
As often as I should . . .

It's because I hope that,
Deep down inside,
You know I do.

— Lisa Wiggett

My Dear Sister

My love and friendship for you
have become so dear to me . . .
I want to hold a place in your heart
as you hold one in mine,
whether we are on separate ends
    of God's earth
    or close together;
let us not grow apart
or let any separation
too large to bridge
    ever come between us;
time passes too quickly
    to spend it on anything
    but well-being . . .

Dearest of friends,
I hope that you will be
happy with every moment of life,
    every breath,
    every touch,
    every sight, smell and sound.
This is my wish of happiness for you,
and my way of saying
"I love you."
May your dreams
    never disappear with age,
but may they continue
as alive and as beautiful as you
with the knowledge that they
will someday come true.

— Joanne Domenech

The love
of a family
is so
uplifting.

The warmth
of a family
is so
comforting.

The support
of a family
is so reassuring.

The attitude
of a family
towards
each other
molds one's
attitude forever
towards the
world.

— Susan Polis Schutz

Sometimes when I am
   really down, and nobody
seems to be my friend
I think of you,
   and the gentlest eyes
      I've ever seen,
   the warmest smile,
   the most accepting heart
I think of what you mean to me
and before long . . .
the skies of living
are clear again
and the sun of hope
is warm.

— Mary Shader

My Sister, My Friend

I think of you
as a very special, dear friend . . .
in a place I hold in my heart
    for just a very few.
You came into my life
    offering happiness,
    with caring underneath.
And I find myself responding
    in the same manner.
It is so easy to talk with you
    about things that sometimes are hard,
    and about things that sometimes I
    have kept well hidden . . .
        even from myself . . .

You seem to be able to draw that out of me,
    and I think that maybe
        I am able to do that for you.
What a beautiful way
        to have
            and build
                a friendship.

— Sue Mitchell

What a wonderful sharing
we have . . .

We share more than a family:
we share a friendship.
There are certain things
we're "supposed" to feel
for each other just because
we're related.

But I know I'd feel those things
and more even if
         we weren't family . . .
No one can understand where
I'm coming from as well as you do.
I guess it's because
         you've been there, too.
And I want you to know . . .
that you're definitely one of my
         favorite people.

— Carol Stewart

There will never exist
between two people
a bond of closeness
or commitment
that is comparable
to the strength
of the ties that bind
you and I.

The years may pass
between us
and time spent apart
may change us . . .

Still the promises made
the lessons learned
the bridges built
and the determination
buried deep within us
will serve only to strengthen
those ever present ties
that bind
you and I.

— Kathy Pepin

Our family

Our feelings of closeness
will never be limited
by the time we spend apart.
Homes and families
as precious as ours
can only be comprised of
    near and caring feelings.
Our family is such an essential
    part of our lives,
that the caring will never leave
    the home,
and the love will reside
    continually in the heart.

— Andrew Tawney

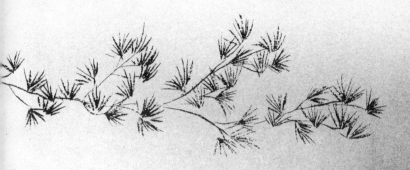

A sister like you . . .

I have my own
    little bit of sunshine
even on the cloudiest days
and my own glowing candle
    to be with me in the dark
I have the most
    wonderful memories
        to think of
and the highest hopes
    for the things still to do

I've got a special,
    precious treasure . . .
because I've got
    a sister like you.

— Laine Parsons

I wish for you
all the usual things one wishes
   for someone they love . . .
      sunshine,
      blue skies,
      and laughter . . .
         lots of laughter.
I wish for you
      happy days
      and smiles
      and all the good things
      one person can wish for
      another.
With all the wishes and
   good intentions,
somehow . . .
it just doesn't seem enough
for someone as uniquely special
as you are.

I love you.
   I'd wish for you the world . . .
   if only it were good enough for you.

— Kathy Pepin

You give so much
   with no thought of being repaid . . .
You give of yourself
through your gifts of
   loving and caring,
   time and acceptance,
   courtesy and kindness.
You share yourself with people —
   your joy, your wealth
And by sharing your blessings
and giving them away,
you create room in your life
   for more blessings
which you so richly deserve.

— Katie Manning

Somehow,
   a simple "thank you"
doesn't really measure up
      to what I'd like
         to say and give . . .
      for everything
         you've given me.
I think, maybe,
      that a rainbow
      or a jar of moonbeams
      would be more appropriate.
I only wish
      I had them to give to you.
Until then, I thank you
from the bottom of my heart.

— Debbie Avery

You are my best friend
because you feel so much
        like home to me . . .
that feeling that someone cares;
that feeling of welcome
that the sight of home
        always brings.

With you as my friend,
I can always know sunshine
        more than my troubles.
You turn any sadness
into a simple understanding
        that I can accept.
And when I'm feeling happy . . .
and wanting to share everything
that is wonderful to me,
you are there . . . ready to listen.

You add so much
to each day . . .
and I wanted to say "thanks."

                              — Yvonne

What greater thing
is there
for two human souls
than to feel that they
are joined for life —
to strengthen each other
in all labor,
to rest on each other
in all sorrow,
to minister
to each other
in all pain,
and to be
with each other
in silent
unspeakable memories . . .

— George Eliot

When You and I Are Apart

Sometimes I get lonely
    and thinking about you helps
reminding me that there is
    a person
I cherish so very much
    always close in spirit
    even when you're
    so far away . . .

But sometimes it hurts
     even more
   to think of you . . .
   your laugh, your touch
   and to remember just
How much I miss
   your gentle face
   your tender ways
   your presence in my life

— Laine Parsons

Thinking of home
Thinking of the past
Thinking of tomorrow
Brings me closer to you
You are a special person
who brings lasting joy
into my life

— Louise Bradford Lowell

Thanks for listening
Thanks for caring
Thanks for always helping
   in times of need
Thanks for sharing
Thanks, sister . . .
   for always being there

— Miles M. Hutchinson

Always, sister

...Remember me,
as I do you,
with all the tenderness
which it is possible for one
to feel for another,
which no time can obliterate,
no distance alter,
but which is always the same.

— Abigail Adams

A "Thank You" to a special sister

There are so many things
that I've never said to you —
things that I've never been able to say
    or never had the perfect opportunity . . .
but I've always wanted you to know that
you've given my life so much . . .

There are times when you've trusted me
    and been forgiving, understanding,
there are times, so many times,
when you made me feel
that I was worth something as a person . . .

You deserve so much thanks,
but it's really not the kind
        that I can repay —
you've done so much already in life,
I don't know that I could add to
the wealth of love and compassion
        that you already hold.

But I do know that
if there's anything
that I can ever do for you —
    all you have to do is ask,
and I'll try my best
    and I'll give my best
and I'll always want the best . . .
    for you.

            — Andrew Tawney

ACKNOWLEDGMENTS

We gratefully acknowledge the permission granted by the following authors, publishers and authors' representatives to reprint poems and excerpts from their publications.

Janice Lamb for "My Sister, My Forever Friend," by Janice Lamb. Copyright © Janice Lamb, 1982. All rights reserved. Reprinted by permission.

Jean Therese for "I ask myself," by Jean Therese. Copyright © Jean Therese, 1981. All rights reserved. Reprinted by permission.

E. Lori Milton for "For my sister," by E. Lori Milton. Copyright © E. Lori Milton, 1982. All rights reserved. Reprinted by permission.

Marilyn Wallace Luff for "I am thankful," by Marilyn Wallace Luff. Copyright © Marilyn Wallace Luff, 1981. All rights reserved. Reprinted by permission.

Jan Kirkley Boyd for "I wanted you to know," by Jan Kirkley Boyd. Copyright © Jan Kirkley Boyd, 1982. All rights reserved. Reprinted by permission.

Susan Staszewski for "Sometimes the pressures of life," by Susan Staszewski. Copyright © Susan Staszewski, 1982. All rights reserved. Reprinted by permission.

Doris Amundson Arnold for "It is comforting," by Doris Amundson Arnold. Copyright © Doris Amundson Arnold, 1981. All rights reserved. Reprinted by permission.

Ronda Scott for "If ever you need to talk," by Ronda Scott. Copyright © Ronda Scott, 1982. All rights reserved. Reprinted by permission.

Jacqueline J. Hancock for "I'd like to capture a rainbow," by Jacqueline J. Hancock. Copyright © Jacqueline J. Hancock, 1982. All rights reserved. Reprinted by permission.

Kathy Boss for "When the world closes in," by Kathy Boss. Copyright © Kathy Boss, 1982. All rights reserved. Reprinted by permission.

Sheryll Anne Sneade for "We may take different steps," by Sheryll Anne Sneade. Copyright © Sheryll Anne Sneade, 1982. All rights reserved. Reprinted by permission.

Debbie Avery for "My Family . . ," by Debbie Avery. Copyright © Debbie Avery, 1982. And for "Somehow," by Debbie Avery. Copyright © Debbie Avery, 1981. All rights reserved. Reprinted by permission.

Lisa Wiggett for "The time I have with you," by Lisa Wiggett. Copyright © Lisa Wiggett, 1982. All rights reserved. Reprinted by permission.

Joanne Domenech for "My love and friendship for you," by Joanne Domenech. Copyright © Joanne Domenech, 1981. All rights reserved. Reprinted by permission.

Mary Shader for "Sometimes when I am really down," by Mary Shader. Copyright © Mary Shader, 1982. All rights reserved. Reprinted by permission.

Sue Mitchell for "I think of you," by Sue Mitchell. Copyright © Sue Mitchell, 1981. All rights reserved. Reprinted by permission.

Carol Stewart for "We share more than a family," by Carol Stewart. Copyright © Carol Stewart, 1981. All rights reserved. Reprinted by permission.

Kathy Pepin for "There will never exist" and "I wish for you," by Kathy Pepin. Copyright © Kathy Pepin, 1982. All rights reserved. Reprinted by permission.

Katie Manning for "You give so much," by Katie Manning. Copyright © Katie Manning, 1982. All rights reserved. Reprinted by permission.

Yvonne for "You are my best friend," by Yvonne. Copyright © Yvonne, 1982. All rights reserved. Reprinted by permission.

A careful effort has been made to trace the ownership of poems used in this anthology in order to obtain permission to reprint copyrighted material and to give proper credit to the copyright owners.

If any error or omission has occurred, it is completely inadvertent, and we would like to make corrections in future editions provided that written notification is made to the publisher: BLUE MOUNTAIN PRESS, INC., P.O. Box 4549, Boulder, Colorado 80306.